D0484800

# The Pocket Coach for Parents

Your Two-Week Guide to a Dramatically
Improved Life with Your Intense Child

# The Pocket Coach for Parents

**Your Two-Week Guide to a Dramatically
Improved Life with Your Intense Child**

**Tina Feigal, M.S.,Ed.
Parent and Teacher Coach**

**www.nurturedheart.com for professionals**

**www.parentingmojo.com for parents and childcare providers**

Acknowledgements:
Special thanks go out to my coaching clients, without whom I would never have learned the techniques developed for this work. I would also like to thank Joe Moses, PhD, my mentor on this project. His support has been enormously helpful and his insights have been right on! And to my editor, Jennifer Manion, PhD: it's amazing how quickly trust can develop when the input is so professional, timely, and informed. I also extend sincere thanks to Milt Adams for his passion for writers, and for the format for bringing their work to the public. I also extend sincere thanks to designer John Toren, who worked quickly, professionally, and compassionately on the final design of this work. My heartfelt appreciation goes out to all of you!

ISBN 10: 1-59298-237-9
ISBN 13: 978-1-59298-237-0
Library of Congress Control Number 2008904105

Printed in the United States of America
First Printing 2007
Second Printing 2008
Third Printing 2009
Fourth Printing 2011
11          6 5 4
Beaver's Pond Press
7104 Ohms Lane, Suite 101
Edina Minnesota, 55439-2129
www.BeaversPondPress.com

*This book is dedicated with love*

*to my sons and teachers,*

*Ben, Jordan, and Jacob*

# Table of Contents

**9**   **Introduction**

**11**   **Chapter One – The Overview**

11   Understanding the Child's Brain

12   Why Doesn't Punishment Work?

13   No Guilt

13   The Child as an Organism

14   The New Way

15   Creating the Energy Match on the "Good Stuff"

15   The Parent as Healer

16   Consistency: The Supreme Challenge

18   When Should I Teach My Values?

22   Using Role Play and Do-Overs to Teach Better Behavior

24   This Takes a Lot of My Energy: How Do I Avoid Burnout?

**28**   **Chapter Two – Your Two-Week Guide**

28   Day One: Get Your Mind Ready

29   Day Two: Begin to Download Successes
     "When you___ I feel___ because___" statements

31   Day Three: The Family Meeting and Rules

37   Day Four: Instituting Breaks for Infractions

38   Day Five: Heartfelt Appreciation Revisited

39   Day Six: Keeping It Positive

39   Day Seven: Ways to Remind Yourself
     to Use the Techniques

40   Day Eight: Teaching Your Child a Lesson

40   Day Nine: Having Your Child Eavesdrop
     as a Parenting Tool

41   Day Ten: Notice Your Own Success

41   Day Eleven: Internalizing Successes

42   Day Twelve: "Testing: One, Two, Three"

43   Day Thirteen: Loving the Child You Have:
     Grown-Up Tasks

44   Day Fourteen: Hold the Child's Success in Your Heart

**46    Chapter Three – Continuing Past the First Two Weeks**

46    The Point System
47    The Credit Chart
51    Points Earned at School
52    Seven Benefits of Present-Moment Parenting
53    Encouragement for You

**55    Chapter Four – Troubleshooting Real Life Challenges**

55    Dealing with Resistance
56    What If She Refuses to Take a Break?
57    What If There is an All-Out Tantrum?
58    Dealing with Oppositional Behaviors—Avoiding Triggers
61    Transforming the Difficult Bedtime
64    Present-Moment Parenting with Teens
66    Preventing Kids from Being Over-Scheduled
69    What Your Child Can't Tell You
70    When Your Child Lies
73    Look for Sensory Integration Issues
74    A Loving Mom's Victory

**80    Chapter Five – Using Restorative Justice**

**85    Resources for Parents**

**87    Personal Parent Coaching For Your Use**

87    Downloading Powerful Successes
90    Additional Exercises for Communicating Values
94    Making Heartfelt Appreciation Effective
96    Earning/Spending Credit Chart
99    Daily Reminder Slips
105   Broke a Rule Notes

**111   About the Author**

# Introduction

Emily is on the phone, telling me of her plight with her nine-year-old. "I am at the end of my rope. My daughter is headed for danger if this behavior keeps up. I have tried everything I know to get her to comply, but nothing works! She is defiant at every turn, and last night she got physical with me when I told her she couldn't bake cookies at 9 p.m. She was hitting, pulling my hair, kicking, and trying to bite me. I am starting to feel afraid of my own child!"

If you are the parent of an intense child, you likely find that the traditional discipline techniques have simply not worked. Repeating yourself (nicely and not-so-nicely), making your voice louder, adding emotion to your interactions, forcing the child to his or her room, grounding, and restricting other freedoms, have actually made the situation worse. Every time you try a new tactic, the child raises the bar and matches or exceeds your level of intensity with her own.

With this guidebook, you will learn how to gain control of your child's behavior using proven techniques that avoid the previous pitfalls. We will use the techniques from my own *Present-Moment Parenting*, which provides a jump-start in applying principles from Howard Glasser's book, *Transforming the Difficult Child: The Nurtured Heart Approach.*

In his book, Glasser develops the concept that providing emotional energy to the child when things are going well is much more effective in improving behavior than most parents' usual response: providing energy when things are going poorly. Using

*The Pocket Coach For Parents,* you will learn to replace your old role as the

## Behavior Police

reacting intensely to unwanted behavior, with a new role as

## Success Mentor

putting yourself in the proactive mode. Your child's behavior will reflect your new approach in a surprisingly positive way.

You will also learn to employ the awesome power of the present moment, which, when one considers it, is all we really have. The past is gone, and the future is not yet here. Present-moment parenting concentrates on avoiding using past experiences to predict future ones, while harnessing the *incredible power of this very moment* to influence future moments.

✶

This book is written with caring and support for parents, care-givers, grandparents, and all who love and care for children whose behavior can best be described as "intense." They are children, ages two to eighteen, who have diagnoses such as ADHD, oppositional defiant disorder, attachment disorder, obsessive compulsive disorder, gifted and talented, or any other of a variety of conditions. They can just be hard to handle, or perhaps are simply going through phases. The techniques included here apply to every child, so your intense one won't feel singled out. As a parent coach, I offer you this book with hope, the real hope I regularly see on the faces and hear in the voices of my caring, loving, newly empowered clients.

## Chapter One

# The Overview: Where Does Intense Behavior Come From?

## Understanding the Child's Brain

The brain of an intense child is equally intense. If we could see the child's brain using technology called a positron emission tomography (PET) scan, we would note that the activity within the brain is less organized, faster, and more intense than that of the average brain. This is helpful to know, as we can now work with this information to create a situation that improves the child's behavior.

This intense brain is looking for a match, just as we do when we fall in love or meet a new friend. We see reflections of ourselves in the other people and are drawn to them. We want to spend as much time as we can with them. When we do, our brains are experiencing highly rewarding matches at subconscious levels. Our togetherness is strongly reinforced, and we are compelled to repeat it.

A similar thing happens within the intense child's brain. But rather than a romantic match, it is looking for an intensity match, attempting to make the exterior environment match the interior brain's level of intensity. The child seeks to stir things up, creating emotional explosions all around her. The brain is hungry for this match, and that is why it appears that she seeks negative attention. No child really seeks negativity from the adults in her world, but her brain is almost addicted to an energy match. This matching urge is something the child is not consciously sensing, a fact which frees us from blaming the child for negative behavior. (We all know from experience how effective the judge-blame-punish cycle is.) Whenever the intensity from the external environment matches the intensity of the internal environment (brain), a reward occurs, and the behavior is likely to be repeated.

This general tendency isn't unique to intense children. We are all looking for intensity matches. If you are a calm person, you want a calm *exterior* environment to match your calm *interior* environment. So how do we put a stop to the string of emotional explosions? We endeavor to **help the intensity match occur when things are going well,** rather than when an infraction has just occurred. Instead of rewarding negative behavior, we want to **reward the positive behavior in this present moment.**

## Why Doesn't Punishment Work?

Both personal experience and Psychology 101 tells us that punishment doesn't work. If you find yourself repeatedly punishing a child for the same behavior, your efforts are not working and it's time to try something new. Punishment does three things. First, it bring us **temporary relief** from negative behavior. However, we are looking for a more permanent resolution. The second effect of punishment is that it creates a perceived need for **retaliation.** The child may not retaliate immediately, but may save up the payback for an unexpected time. This is when we often see negative behavior or tantrums "out of the blue." Again, the child is not seeking to be bad, but the brain keeps a scorecard of intensity, which appears to **require** equilibrium. Whenever the child is punished, a little marker gets left inside his head and heart, compelling him to respond by making the score even. This is, again, something about which the child is not conscious. The third effect of punishment is creating **fear**. However, most parents would rather base their relationships with their children on love and support than on fear, and so punishing is less than ideal.

Cast blame aside, and just see the child as an organism responding to his environment. Work to leave **a marker of success** in his brain and heart whenever possible, encouraging messages like: "I am a good kid," "I can please these people," or "I can do the right thing." A child with these internal affirmations does not *need* to look for energy around negativity. The intensity is around the good behaviors, so the brain will seek its match there.

## No Guilt

It is utterly understandable if you have been punishing your child's negative behavior up to this point. It may have been the only tool you had in your tool bag to stop negative behavior. Many of us were raised with this perspective, and in fact, much of our society is based upon looking for infractions and punishing for them. However, this is not effective with intense children and, in fact, punishment makes the behavior worse. Its other effect is to set the child on a journey of progressively limited freedoms that starts at home with small behavior restrictions, and continues at school with detention, then suspension, and possibly expulsion. The natural sequence of these events leads too many children to the juvenile justice system, and eventually adult detention and prison. We can stop this self-perpetuating cycle by intervening now, using the present moment to help the child form a whole new self-image that leads the child to affirm, **"I am successful and worthy of positive feedback."**

## The Child as an Organism: Understanding the Effect of Your Input on His Heart

At the Institute of Heartmath (IHM), researchers discovered a very helpful finding: **the heart is responsive to emotional input**. Literally, this is something we see in poetry and love songs, but now scientists can see that **the rhythm of the heartbeat changes** when emotion is "downloaded" into the heart. When we download any emotionally charged message, positive or negative, we actually have an emotion-generated **physiological** effect, not unlike blushing. Matching the child-brain intensity with a positive comment causes a similar reaction. Maybe you have noticed what a child looks like when you really "hit home" with a compliment or affirmation. You may say something like, "When you were speaking so politely to Ms. Harrison at school yesterday, it just made me feel SO proud of you!" The child's eyes turn downward, he tries not to smile, and he maybe even gets a little teary. Or maybe he beams from ear to ear. Those are physiological responses!

Another IHM discovery is that the heart has its own neurological system that sends messages to the brain. So as mentioned earlier, when we give children our input, we create and strengthen the heart-to-brain neural pathway that says, "I am a good kid. I can do the right thing. I can please my parents and teacher. I am successful." Alternatively, our input can also deliver the heart-brain message, "I am not a good kid. I can never do the right thing. I am a failure." **We have a choice about what to download into the child.** It's our job as adults to shape the future by using this moment to give his heart the sustenance it needs to grow and become the heart it was meant to be. The child is an organism, just like a plant. If we put the plant in the sunlight and give it water and fertilizer, it grows to become the plant it was intended to be. If we put it in the closet and shut the door, it withers, turns brown, and dies. If we deliver negative messages to the child, he or she will turn sour and become anxious, depressed, and oppositional. If we deliver the sunshine of heartfelt appreciation, the rain of clarity, and the nutrients of values shared when there is no infraction, the organism will grow and blossom into the child it was destined to be.

## The New Way

Our strategy now changes from giving a "reward" of emotional energy (intensity demonstrated by wide eyes, loud voices, and big gestures) for **unwanted** behavior, to delivering emotional rewards for **desired** behavior. This seems simple enough, but its practical application has its challenges. As adults we are so programmed to respond to negative behavior in order to teach children lessons that we need to exert significant effort to put our emphasis elsewhere. The good thing about emphasizing the positive is that it really works. Not only will it dramatically improve the child's behavior, but it's also so rewarding to you personally that your sense of yourself as a parent will take a huge leap forward.

## Creating the Energy Match on the "Good Stuff"

Whenever something goes right, add intensity to your positive comment by saying

"When you____I feel____because____."

This becomes the equivalent of yelling, by creating a much more emotionally charged message than does the typical "thanks" or "good job." We are looking for a very large download that creates an energy match for the child's brain. We want to cause a strong emotional reaction, just as yelling does, only on the positive side. Using "When you ___ I feel ___ because ___" serves the purpose well. We'll refer to it here as "heartfelt appreciation."

## The Parent as Healer

Applying Present-Moment Parenting to controlling children's challenging behaviors is the best way to bring about the healing you desire. This model employs the power of the relationship between you and the child, where love and connection already exist. PMP is perfect in that it can be woven into the child's life twenty-four hours a day, seven days a week, rather than for an hour a week, which happens with typical therapy. Also, the intense child is often not likely to respond well to a therapist's questions about feelings and motivation. When the child answers a therapist's queries with "I don't know," she is telling the truth. She doesn't understand the workings of her intensity-hungry brain as it looks for a match in the environment. But we as adults can help her brain locate **where the intensity is** and **where it is not,** and bring about the changes we desire for the child and for ourselves. Am I saying that traditional therapy never helps? No. But I have found that if a child is in therapy, PMP is a powerful adjunct that supports parents and helps kids get better.

## Consistency: The Supreme Challenge

I often hear from parents that they have a hard time staying consistent with their children. They are tired, hurried, hassled, and worn out. They just want their child to behave, but the harder they try to gain cooperation, the worse the situation becomes. How does a parent stay with the child whose brain is seeking intensity without "losing it" on a regular basis? With Present-Moment Parenting, it's easier to stay in what I call "the parent place" than you think. First, get your mind set in advance. Do a little mental run-through of the last altercation with your child. See yourself responding calmly, with a simple, "Broke a rule. Take a break." Then visualize the next infraction. See yourself responding this way again. Remind yourself to let go of the past, with all of its tirades, tantrums, hurtful words, and negotiations, as it is over and cannot be changed.

**The present is all you have, so use it to your best advantage.** Eckhardt Tolle, the author of the book *The Power of Now*, points out that nothing has ever happened in the past, and nothing will ever happen in the future. Everything happens in the present moment. Make this very moment with the child in front of you the best it can be by responding in a positive way, and the future will take care of itself. Work to release earlier scenarios in order to create new ones. Your interactions with your child will all be aimed at the goal of turning negative behavior around. No energy flows to him when things are going poorly, but copious energy flows to him when rules are not being broken, and when behavior is appreciated.

★

**Note:** The definition of insanity is repeating the same thing over and over and expecting different results. If you have tried your old techniques many times with little or no improvement, it's time for a change. Also, take note of whether your child is repeating the behavior and expecting different results. Teach him not to do this. Employ direct teaching by rehearsing better responses to frustrating situations, so that he can grow in his social interactions by actually feeling his body and mind having an appropriate response.

## Exercise:

Use this moment to check in with your child. Is there something occurring right now that you can reward with your heartfelt appreciation? Do it. Come back and record it here.

---

---

---

---

Consistency comes not from doling out strict discipline when things are going poorly, but from making a decision about your reaction in advance, and rehearsing the improved scene while there is no issue. When you have decided to stay in the parent place and never waver from your plan, half the battle is won. You can now remain solid in your position, and no amount of whining, threatening, arguing, throwing, bullying, swearing, or "I-hate-you"s will change it. You are certain that you will always give your child what he needs: heartfelt appreciation when things are going well, and a break when they are not. This is the most loving combination you can offer. You win because you have eliminated the guilt of inconsistency, while feeling secure in your stance. The child wins because she knows what your responses will be. This creates the predictability and security she craves.

Please note that children crave a high energy match while at the same time they crave predictability and security. This is simply the nature of children. While they attempt to gain mastery over their interactions, parts of their development are not in sync with other parts. So yes, children often crave intensity, and also need a great deal of security to help them learn appropriate responses. Think of predictablility as the stage upon which they develop their skills, and energy matching for good behavior as the acting method you are teaching.

All of this translates into a deep love that transforms the former state of upheaval and anxiety. Your daily life with your child can now be much more enjoyable, calm, and serene. Surely there will be some backsliding, and certainly you'll see some testing, but your consistent response, based on your **pre-determined reaction to unwanted behavior,** will bring things back into focus very quickly. Staying in the parent place is now your preferred way of being, reinforced every day by the improvements you see in your child.

## When Should I Teach My Values?

As parents we usually try to impart our values at the time when the child is least receptive: when there has just been an infraction. We can lecture all we want at this time, but the child doesn't absorb one bit of the message. The emotions are running too high, and the words just don't sink in.

The best time to teach values is when there has been no infraction and things are going well. Use the dinner table, travel time, tuck-in time, videos, TV, relationship issues that you encounter, your daily life with bosses, co-workers, and relatives, all the regular incidents of life, as occasions to share your values. Even if what happened in life or what was on TV conflicts with your values, grab the opportunity to critique it to teach your child what you want him to know now, while you have him in the learning laboratory of your family. Time is precious, and kids grow up so fast. So many lessons need to be learned, and although you may not always feel it, your time together is limited. Use your present moment.

Here's an example: when the child looks about to engage in a full-blown tantrum or attack, **get there first.** Use the present moment to create a success from the fact that he hasn't said any bad words, even if you think he would have in the next moment. Seek every opportunity to download a positive message into your child's mind and heart, even if you have to fudge a bit. It's worth your time and effort, and it helps him realize he is being success-ful right now, even if just for a millisecond. When you get there first, you maximize the present and begin to build a foundation of successes. From there, you can use present moments to talk about past successes, continuing to reinforce what you want by teaching your values here and now.

## Exercise:

Write three of your family's values. Examples are: honesty, good manners, neatness, and respectful language.

1._____

2._____

3._____

Describe how you most recently communicated these three values to your child(ren). Note whether you did this at the time of an infraction, or when things were calm.

1. The value:_____

How I communicated it:_____

_____

When I communicated:\_\_\_\_\_After the infraction
\_\_\_\_\_When things were calm

2. The value:_____

How I communicated it:_____

_____

When I communicated: \_\_\_\_\_After the infraction
\_\_\_\_\_When things were calm

3. The value:_____

_____

How I communicated it:_____

_____

When I communicated: \_\_\_\_\_After the infraction
\_\_\_\_\_When things were calm

Now make a plan for sharing your three values at the best possible time, when things are going well. Think about using the present moment to your best advantage. Use TV, travel time, movies, or life experiences as the context for a constructive, enjoyable conversation. These may be from yesterday or last week. Definitely feel free to discuss them after the fact, as mentioned above, to strengthen the teaching of your values.
Write your plans on the space provided below:

1._____

_____

2._____

_____

3._____

_____

To help you get the conversation started, here are some phrases to use:

- "I was just thinking of that time last week when my cousin Sara called to tell me about her son. Remember, he got into trouble at school? Let's talk about how we would handle his situation in our family."

**Note:** Use of the phrase "in our family" is powerful in its ability to create and expand your family identity. This fulfills a need that is basic to every human being: **belongingness** (from Abraham Maslow's hierarchy of needs.) Use "in our family" whenever you can.

- "You were so wonderful yesterday when Adam called to ask you over to his house. You told him you had to check with me, which I really appreciate. You are really learning how to get what you need in such a respectful way!"

With this comment you have:

- *shown your heartfelt appreciation with a "When you___I feel ___ because___" statement*
- *taught your value (obeying the "ask permission" rule) directly*
- *downloaded a big success into the child, sending the heart-to-brain message, "I am a good kid. I can do the right thing."*
- *increased the likelihood that it, or something equally positive, will happen again*

- "When you fed the dog this morning, I was thinking about how she depends on you for so much—you play with her, you let her out, you throw the ball with her, and you feed her! What would that dog do without you?"

With this comment, you have:

- *shared your values about taking care of a pet*
- *shown your heartfelt appreciation*

21

- *downloaded a success into the child's mind and heart*
- *increased his sense of being a caretaker in a healthy way*
- *increased the likelihood of this behavior, or something even better, occurring again*

## Using Role Play and Do-Overs to Teach Better Behavior

Another wonderful tool for bringing out the best in children is to role play troublesome situations. Let's say your child comes home with a story about how a kid on the bus took his hat and threw it. Your child got angry and went after the other kid, and was promptly reported to the principal for misbehaving on the bus. This is the third time it's happened, and you can see the handwriting on the wall: soon your child will be banned from the bus.

The best way to teach your child what you want him to know is to replay the scene, helping him come up with a response that does not get him into trouble. (This is a great stance to take: "I just don't want to see you getting into trouble any more.") Decide who should be your child and who should be the other kid. Rehearse the scene exactly as he said it happened, disregarding whether it is absolutely "true." The important thing is his perception of the scene, as this is what is true for him. Replay the scene with a better response, such as ignoring the kid who threw the hat, and asking for the hat as you leave the bus. Then trade roles, so your child can be in the other child's shoes, too, which broadens his perspective on the scene. (This is especially good for kids who need help developing empathy.)

Role playing every scene you want to see improved is a powerful way to "build a map in the child's brain" for the way things can occur. Being young, kids often don't realize they have alternatives to fighting back or lashing out when someone annoys them. Role playing gives them that alternative in a very real way. It only takes a few moments, and is a powerful method for teaching the child's body a new response to conflict. It's also fun! If the child doesn't understand the alternative response right away, just repeat the role playing until it sinks in.

Another powerful tool for bringing out the best in kids is the "do-over." If your child whines, for example, you can ask for a "do-over" so that she can learn to speak in a tone that your ears can accept. Rehearse this at a time when there is no infraction, so that the learning can readily occur.

You: "Let's figure out how to get rid of some of the whining in this house. You know how I am always saying, 'No whining'?" The child will be relieved that you're aware that you're often correcting her about this.

You: "I'll whine and you say 'do-over,' and then I'll ask for what I want in a better tone of voice. 'Moooommmm, can I go over to Emily's....pleeeeeeeease? Moooommmm, I said I want to go to Emileeeee's. Listen to meeeeeee."

Child: "Do-over!"

You: "Mom, is it OK if I go to Emily's?" in a normal tone of voice. This teaches the child to state things in a tone to which others can respond without feeling frustrated. Then switch roles, so that your child can learn from both perspectives how the exchange should sound.

And be sure that, when your child later uses a tone you can accept, you respond to her as quickly as possible with heartfelt appreciation. "I love that tone of voice, Honey! It shows me that you really know how to get a person's attention!" You have now assured yourself of less whining, and you've both had fun creating a new way of doing things!

## This Takes a Lot of My Energy:
## How Do I Avoid Burnout?

Present-moment parenting may seem daunting. It requires preparation, practice, vigilance, and the mastering of specific skills. It may also seem to require that parents forego their own needs beyond those of controlling their intense child. But this need not be the case. In fact, it's vital to pay attention to your own needs on a regular basis in order to successfully implement present-moment parenting.

When we travel by air, we hear the phrase, "Place the mask over your own mouth and nose first, and then assist others." This is a powerful metaphor for parenting in today's world. It illustrates the need for self-preservation when facing the enormous task of raising a challenging child. Most of the parents with whom I work have very little concept of self-preservation. They are like hamsters in cages, reacting to whatever comes, with no "big picture" plan for sustaining themselves. What lies beneath this is a belief that they should somehow fill others' cups without filling their own. Or they may just be trying to stay ahead of their child's next impulse. Certainly one can provide for someone else for the short run, ignoring one's personal needs. But this doesn't work for a sustained period of time without great cost to the mental, and often physical, well-being of the parent.

### Exercise:

On the next page describe a recent incident in which you let your own needs go while attempting to restore peace, or correct your child's impulsive negative behavior.

Example: You gave in to your child and bought something for him that you thought was extravagant. Your values were interfered with, and it was a hit to your sense of yourself as a competent money manager.

Now imagine that you had applied the principles of "placing the mask over your own mouth first." Give your child the loving, predictable consequences he needs while maintaining your own composure and financial wisdom. Re-write the incident here.

_____

_____

_____

_____

_____

_____

_____

_____

_____

_____

_____

_____

_____

_____

_____

_____

_____

_____

_____

_____

_____

## My Progress Notes

Obstacles to implementing the ideas in this chapter:

Ways I will overcome the obstacles:

My success story:

*Chapter Two*

# Your Two-Week Guide
# to a Dramatically Improved
# Life With Your Intense Child

Here is a day-by-day schedule that you can follow while learning to employ **present-moment parenting.** Use it strictly as a guide. If your Day One lasts a week, so be it. The important thing is to give yourself time to adjust your interactions with your challenging child at your perfect pace. Trust your instincts.

## DAY ONE
## Get Your Mind Ready

Prepare yourself mentally to help your child change her behavior by just **starting to notice your child's tiny successes.** This is more than catching kids being good. Notice when your child follows rules. Use the image of Howard Glasser's Shamu story, in which he examines how a nineteen-ton whale learns to jump over a rope twenty-two feet above the surface of the tank at Sea World. The trainers first place the rope on the bottom of the pool, then reward "underwater rope crossing behavior," and then raise the rope incrementally until Shamu is thrilling the crowds with dramatic acrobatics. Do the same for your child: find the success in the ordinary present moments. Do not say anything yet; just notice.

## DAY TWO
### Begin to Download Successes

Take three or four opportunities today to give heartfelt appreciation to your child. Use the present moment to stop and take stock. Is there something happening right now that you appreciate? Is there a tiny moment of peace and quiet (remember, your brain is looking for an intensity match, too, and the level it wants is "low!"). Is the child behaving in such a way that could be construed as positive, such as speaking in an indoor voice, keeping his hands to himself, or holding still? Even if it's happening for a nanosecond, **get there first,** and download a success into the child's heart.

Use your three-part statement of heartfelt appreciation:

**"When you___ I feel___ because___."**

For example:

- "When you put your plate in the dishwasher, I was extremely proud of you because it shows me how grown up you are!"

- "When you played nicely with the baby, I was so touched. I can tell how sensitive you are to her needs."

- "When you spoke to my cousin on the phone just now, you were so polite, and just handed the phone right to me. Do you know what you did? You built a bridge between Janelle and me! Thank you so much!"

Remember, these three-part statements are the **emotional impact equivalent of yelling.** They land more firmly in the child's mind and heart than do "Good job answering the phone," and "Thanks for putting your plate in the dishwasher."

**More examples are on the next page.**

# Making Heartfelt Appreciation Very Effective
## Downloading Powerful Successes by Including Feeling Language

| When you... | I feel... | because... |
| --- | --- | --- |
| clean up | rested | it helps mom's day go better |
| tell me about your social events | close to you | you share your life with me |
| say "OK" when I ask you something | relieved | there's no screaming |
| go to bed when asked | listened to | I don't have to ask more than once |
| control your strong feelings | my heart gets so big | you worked hard to help us get along |
| put your hat and coat on | so excited | we get Sister to school on time |
| surprise me by doing your chores | important and loved | I know you are trying to do well |
| help your brother with a game | respected | you are listening to my request |
| hang up your jacket | appreciative | we don't have to pick up after you |
| share your toys | proud | I see the generous person you are |
| start homework w/o being told | excited | we'll get to do other things together |

Pat yourself on the back. You have started the physiological change in your child's body by downloading success into her brain and heart. With repetition, the heart-to-brain neural pathway that says "I am a good kid," or "I'm sensitive to the needs of others" will be strengthened. And you will see that the behavior of the child who thinks of herself this way is dramatically improved, over the behavior of the child who thinks she can never do anything right.

## DAY THREE
## The Family Meeting and Rules

Make a plan for a family meeting. Collaborate with your spouse or another trusted adult, or decide to do it on your own. Determine a time and day that works for you and your family members. Sunday evening at 6 p.m. is a common family meeting time. Plan to meet every week or more often if situations come up. Or you may just meet because you enjoy this process.

Each family member is free to call a family meeting when he sees a need. It doesn't have to be a serious thing, and in fact, the lighter it is, the better it is for the kids. They'll respond much better to something that involves fun than to a heavy-feeling encounter. Incorporate snacks, too, so that the meeting feels casual enough for the kids' comfort.

### Read the following in advance of
### holding the family meeting:

Organizations of all types, including churches, companies, and clubs, meet to discuss their processes. I often wonder why the exception to this rule is the family, the most important unit of society, and the one upon which all societal success depends. It's time to institute regular family meetings so that families can be as strong as other organizations.

In keeping with the spirit of present-moment parenting, hold meetings to lift up the children by pointing out the whole family's successes. And when there is an issue that needs the family's attention, use the resource of the wisdom of each family member to resolve it.

## Holding a Successful Family Meeting

**1. Invite the children to the meeting,** showing the same respect for them that you would for an adult. If the children aren't available due to homework, etc., ask for an alternative time. Buy-in increases when the children are respected and feel they have a voice in the process. If they don't want to come to the meeting, do not insist. Hold it anyway, and watch how they get pulled in by curiosity. They will eventually get used to meetings as the "family norm," especially when they realize that the meetings are pleasant and that the children will have a valuable voice in the process.

**2. State that the purpose of the meeting** is to decide together how things are going in the family, to share successes, and to make improvements where necessary.

**3. a) Use a talking piece,** a symbol that grants that the person holding it the right to speak his or her mind without being interrupted. It should have some significance for the whole family. It could be a statue, a photo of all of you, or a memento from a family vacation. The family may even want to create a new talking piece as a shared activity.

**b) Whoever has the talking piece speaks, and whoever doesn't have the talking piece listens.**
Listening is such a vital component to living a successful adult life. It's amazing how little focus it receives and how little training we get in it. Use this opportunity to teach your children what you want them to know about listening. When you notice them listening, say, "I noticed you are listening very well! I bet you can even tell me what your brother just said." Then listen carefully as your child repeats what he heard, and follow with

heartfelt appreciation for listening so well. "You did hear what your sister said! I knew you were a great listener!"

**c) The speaker continues speaking until completely finished,** rather than being rushed to finish so others can speak. (This takes the pressure to finish off the speaker, and removes the conflict over the talking piece. It also teaches others patience with the speaker. Allow plenty of time for the first meeting.) Anyone can have the talking piece back when he has something else to say...all within reason, of course.

**4. If you have some issues with interrupting,** have one family member, on a rotating basis, take charge of making sure that the listeners listen while the speaker speaks. If the monitor is one of the children, be sure to deliver your heartfelt appreciation for a job well done.

**5. Devote the entire first meeting to what you love about being in the family,** and then **end the meeting.** This leaves the children with a positive feeling about being contributing members of the family and about participating in meetings. Start each meeting by saying what you love.

**6. At the second meeting,** start by having each person say what they love about being in the family, and then bring up an issue you want resolved. Just describe what takes place without emotion, as if you are reporting the news.

For example:

"Every evening it seems we have a lot of arguing at bedtime. Here's what happens, and tell me if I am getting this right: I say, 'It's time for bed,' and you ignore me. Then my voice gets louder. I say, 'Let's get your pajamas on,' and you leave the room. My voice gets more irritated and I say, 'Time to brush your teeth.' You jump on the bed. I say, 'It's time to pick out a story,' and you run downstairs. My voice gets louder and louder and pretty soon I am nagging you, and in a little while I am yelling. I can tell you one thing ... I hate to yell at you. And I am pretty sure you hate being yelled at. Is that right?" The children will likely respond with a heartfelt "yes!" Continue with: "Let's do what we always do, which is that we always get pajamas on; we always brush teeth; we always read a story; and we always turn off the light, only *without the yelling*. Would you like that?" Again, the kids will likely feel relief, and offer an enthusiastic "yes!" If they give the slightest approval, or even if they don't, just compassionately continue with the meeting.

## The Rules

Then say, "OK, we're going to need a list of rules so we can help our family get along the very best we can. **What should the rules be?**" Having the kids make the rule list increases buy-in to the process. You can act as their secretary and write down what they say, which communicates even more of a feeling of importance to their contributing to the list. After they are finished with the list, **add whatever rules you think still need to be included.** Then point out that **you as the parents reserve the right to make up rules on the spot whenever you see the need.** That way, you won't get into a struggle about enforcing rules that aren't on the list.

**The rules should start with "no."** This is most helpful for intense kids who often have auditory processing issues. (They hear the sounds just fine, but the storage, retrieval, and interpretation of the sounds is not the same as it is for other kids. That's why lengthy explanations are often lost on these kids. It's not that they are not listening, but their brains' processing problems keep them from knowing what the sounds mean.) So a very clear "no interrupting" or "no loud noises" is the best for helping them achieve success in following the rules.

How long should the list be? A list of five to seven rules works well. You'll need more if you have a wide age-range in your family, or perhaps you'll want a big kids' list and a little kids' list. The list is for the whole family, so parents follow the rules just as the kids do. Explain to the kids that the rule list will be revised as necessary. As they grow, the rules will need to change to suit their needs. Regular family meetings will serve this purpose well.

Hold them weekly, but more often if you need to.

**Post the rules at kid-eye level on the refrigerator.** Use writing or pictures, whichever you need for your readers and non-readers. "No parking" signs through pictures of kids yelling, etc., work well. Google has an images tab for your use in this project. Now you can **reward both positive behaviors and the lack of rules being broken.** "I notice when you were playing with Jared just now, you were not shouting. I love how you follow the rules! In fact, I think you are our champion rule-follower!" This is **"time in"** and *it is where your* **true power** *lies* for bringing out positive behavior. You use the power of the present moment to download a success into the child, contributing to the heart-to-brain message, "I am a good kid."

On page 105 you'll find reminder slips to post where you will see them often, so that downloading successes soon becomes a habit. Tape them on the fridge, near the phone, on the bathroom mirror, on your dashboard ... anywhere your eyes frequently land.

## Breaks (Time Outs)

Tell your children that there will be a **break every time a rule is broken.** The breaks will take place in a designated chair in a room in which you are present. (Breaks are thus not banishment to other rooms, nor are they punishments.) **The break begins when the child sits calmly in the break spot.** Therefore, the child can determine when it starts and when it ends. When you explain breaks, say, "The break starts when you are calm in the chair. Once it starts it can end, so you decide when it starts and, therefore, when it ends." (Do not say this at the time of an infraction, but rather, explain the idea of the break within the context of the family meeting.) When a rule is broken, no energy goes to the child, and all privileges are frozen until the break is served. The break lasts thirty seconds. (See "Safe Hold" in Chapter Four for times when the child is a danger to herself or to you.)

You are not talking to the child's moral center at this time, nor are you teaching him a lesson. You only want to convey to his brain that no energy follows his breaking of a rule. He will receive lots of your energy for the good things but no energy for rule-breaking. The energy-hungry brain will learn where to direct its efforts, namely away from infractions and toward behavior that evokes positive intensity, in the form of parents' heartfelt appreciation:

**When you ___ I feel ___ because ___ .**

On page 106 you'll find some reminder notes to cut out and use every time your child does something you don't want him to do. Post them where you are most likely to see them several times a day. Use the notes until this becomes a habit.

**Note:** For preschoolers and many teens, you will use redirection four or five times for every "break." Redirection just means that you lead the child to the better behavior right away, rather than making an issue out of the infraction. This is another way of giving no energy to the infraction. For a preschooler, for example, instead of using a break when he is swinging his feet near the newly-painted living room wall, just suggest using those feet to run around outside: "Look at those swingy feet. They have so much energy! How about taking them outside to see if they need some running time?"

For teens, please see Chapter Four in this book for hints on how to gain their cooperation. Breaks may not be your first choice with older children.

**7. Guard your meeting time as sacred.** If you decide on Sunday at 6 p.m. for your meetings, be sure that you don't let that time commitment erode. Let the children overhear you declining other opportunities to fill that time slot, just as you would decline them because of religious services or important business meetings. It will increase their sense of the importance of the meeting time, as well as the importance of their family identity. As issues come up between meetings, ask family members if they think you need an impromptu meeting. Remind the kids that they can call meetings when they see a need, as well. Your flexibility and inclusive approach also increase buy-in to the meetings and to the solutions that result from your discussion.

**8. Give the children your heartfelt appreciation for their participation in the meeting.** You can say:

"When you participated in our family meeting, I felt like we were really a together group. It was really nice for all of us to find out what great ideas you have!"

## DAY FOUR
## Instituting Breaks for Infractions

Whenever a rule is broken, your ONLY response is **"Broke a Rule. Take a Break."** Give no warnings, engage in no negotiations, and offer no reiteration of the rule. In other words:

**NO** "One more of those and you are going to be taking a break."

**NO** (Child): "If I promise not to do it again, can I not take my break?"

(You): "Oh, all right, but you have to remember next time."

**NO** "That was spitting and you know we have a rule against spitting."

These interactions all give energy to the infraction, which feeds the intensity-hungry brain what it wants most (your emotional energy) and rewards the very behavior you don't want. **All you want to do is stop the behavior with an energy-free break. Rehearse breaks** with your child. As part of the family meeting, allow her body to feel what happens when there is an infraction. For the rehearsal, say to the child:

"OK, say a bad word, and then I'll say 'Broke a Rule. Take a Break.'" After giving you a rather puzzled but interested look, the child says the bad word. You say, "Broke a Rule. Take a Break." The child sits in the designated spot for thirty seconds. You say, "Thank you very much for taking your break so well. Now let's go finish picking up those toys so we can go over to Grandma's house (or whatever is happening next.)"

Here's the "break formula":

1. Infraction  2. Broke a Rule. Take a Break.  3. Thank you very much  4. Redirect. You deliver no judgment, no discussion, no energy to negativity. It's the same as putting out a fire by depriving it of oxygen. You want to extinguish the behavior, so you deprive it of your energy.

Your child will learn several things from this, the first of which is that breaks are not the end of the world. In fact, we can even rehearse them and play around with them a little. Second, she'll learn that Dad can respond to infractions without getting all riled up. And third, she'll now know exactly what will occur if she breaks a rule. That clarity helps her stay within the boundaries. And **if you break a rule,** by yelling or losing your temper, you can set a great example of responding to your own negative behavior by putting yourself in break. Yes, the kids will love that.

## DAY FIVE
### Heartfelt Appreciation Revisited

Continue giving your child small moments of feedback when things are going well.

**"When you ___ I feel ___ because ___"**

**creates the emotional intensity match** that the child's brain desires. Remember: think of it as the equivalent of yelling, only on the positive side. It rewards the brain, so the good behavior will be repeated. Do this at least three times today.

## DAY SIX
### Keeping It Positive

Wake up in the morning and ask yourself, "How can I energize the success of my child today?" (This contrasts your former question, "How will I ever make it through the day with this child?") Pat yourself on the back for taking on this challenge courageously.

Giving energy to the positives you see in the present moment is so far removed from our traditional ways of changing child behavior that it requires a huge effort at the beginning. Trust that it will get easier as you practice, and that the rewards of better behavior will be so compelling that you won't have the slightest desire to return to the old ways.

Energize the child's success at least four times today. If it's a rough day, think in terms of taking and encouraging baby steps; find the tiniest success and reward it with your focused attention. Remember that, **although you could choose to energize negativity by yelling today, you choose to energize positivity by delivering your heartfelt appreciation.** It will get you what you want: good behavior, peace in your relationship, and high self-esteem in your child.


## DAY SEVEN
### Ways to Remind Yourself to Use the Techniques

If you find yourself becoming distracted from giving positive energy to the child, go back to the printed reminders in this book, and place them around the house, car, garage, and yard. If you would like, just write a + (positive) sign on a sticky note, or write "remember," or draw a picture. The symbol can be something that only you know, or it can be something the kids are in on, too. It's up to you, but if the kids are in on it, they may use the notes to remind *themselves* to be positive with you and with each other! Note: If you have a highly sensitive child, you may want to experiment with ways that he or she can accept positive feedback. I suggest writing him notes with "When you___ I feel ___ because ___ " messages on them and placing them under his pillow, or in his backpack for later discovery. If your child isn't reading yet, write the notes anyway, and read them to him at bedtime. This creates a wonderful moment of highly rewarding intimacy, centered on the good behavior you desire. You will definitely see more good behavior.

**Note**: Chapter Four of this book has more on this.

## DAY EIGHT
## Teaching Your Child a Lesson

Look for at least two opportunities to **share your values when there is no infraction** today. When you see something happen between a parent and child or siblings in the grocery store, engage your child in a quiet conversation about how "our family" does things. Remember to use what happens between the neighbors, on TV, during your work day, while driving in traffic, or what you hear in a song on the radio. Take the opportunity to share what good behavior and beliefs look like in your world, and use your family name to identify the values. "In the Jones family, we do it this way." Keep in mind that your time to teach is limited; kids grow up and move on. **Use this time** while they are in the "laboratory" of your home to teach them what you want them to know, and to give them the social skills you want them to have. When they leave home, you will be assured that you have given them what they need to get along in the world.

## DAY NINE
## Having Your Child Eavesdrop as a Parenting Tool

Let the child overhear you discussing her successes in glowing terms with your spouse or another adult. You know how kids have radar for phone conversations? (Why is that, do you suppose? I think it's because they are learning to be adults and to have adult conversations. They need to listen very intently when you are on the phone because they only hear half of the conversation, and need to do a lot of mental processing to imagine the other half.) Use this radar to your greatest advantage to download further successes into the child. Here's an example:

> "Do you know what Gina did today? She played quietly while Evan was taking his nap, and when he woke up, she greeted him with that cute little voice she uses. He was so excited to see her! And I was thrilled to see what a caring big sister she is. Thanks for listening, Mom. I love to tell share the good things with you. Yes, I am really proud of her."

Involving a third party is powerful stuff. It brings about real change by lifting up the child's sense of self in your eyes, as communicated to other people.

## DAY TEN
### Notice Your Own Success

Begin to allow yourself to think, "I am a success at this." Notice **any** successes for which you can take credit. Write them down. Reward yourself by getting a sitter. Pat yourself on the back all the way to the restaurant where you are going for a celebration dinner. Don't put this one off.

## DAY ELEVEN
### Internalizing Successes

Focus on how the successes must feel to the child.

> "Wow, that must feel so wonderful to have three stars on your school chart today! I bet you are feeling pretty darn good about it."

The ultimate goal of present-moment parenting is to use this moment to **infuse the positive messages into the child, so that he eventually internalizes them.**

This gets at a question I often hear: **"Can you praise a child too much?"** When your child's behavior has been very challenging, I believe it is more important to focus on whether the success downloads are frequent enough, rather than whether they are too frequent. Remember that, since the challenging child has had so many negative, punishing downloads that need to be counteracted, it will be quite awhile before the positives will get to be too much. If you start to feel as if they are too frequent, and the child is becoming deaf to them, or they are not having the effect you wanted, back off from giving heartfelt appreciations, but don't stop. Use more of the internalizing suggestions in the paragraph above.

## DAY TWELVE
### "Testing: One, Two, Three"

Children are **scientists.** They are testing to see what stays true over several trials. Develop an appreciation for this persistence, knowing that it will serve them very well as adults. (During coaching sessions, I am often conscious of the fact that I am talking to the parents of future leaders: if we can just get them safely to adulthood!)

Since the child is a scientist who is always testing to see what stays true, your role is clear. Show him that it always stays true that he will hear heartfelt appreciation when he engages in desired behavior. And show him that it always stays true that he will be redirected or have a break when he breaks a rule. Simple enough. The more consistent you are with your heartfelt appreciation, redirection, and requesting of breaks, and the more predictable the results, the sooner the child's experiment can end. The question "What will happen when I do this?" has been answered.

## DAY THIRTEEN
### Loving the Child You HAVE: Grown-Up Tasks

Intense children are constantly getting involved in something. Sometimes it's appropriate, and sometimes it's not. The basic nature of your child, namely that she is curious and always wanting "more," will likely not change. She may be talkative, questioning, opinionated, and insistent. The positive side of these traits is that she will definitely be a "force in the world" as an adult. Today you will focus on **going with your child's natural urges** to get the best behavior out of her. The child's greatest task is to individuate from you, which means becoming "not Mom" and "not Dad," but "me." It's an established fact that you might be successful making a person something she is not, but the chance of her growing up healthy and happy are not great if her major teacher (parent) finds her most authentic self unacceptable.

If you have an artistic child, discover ways that you need his talent (e.g., designing invitations, choosing colors for a room, arranging furniture; whatever his strength may be). And if you have a mechanical child, use her special abilities to help figure out what needs to happen if, for example, the garage door doesn't work. If you have a musical child, have her entertain you and your friends whenever possible, unless she is self conscious about it. (Don't push her to perform if it causes her extreme discomfort. You will never foster growth in her with that tactic. Give her time and space to perform on her terms, which may be only playing for herself or family.) If you have a child that writes well, engage her talents for composing the annual family letter to friends, or have her write a letter to the editor on a topic that interests her.

**Give children grown-up tasks to do** whenever it is feasible. Your aim is to lift the child up to new heights: parents often tell me their children just *glow* when they are given grown-up tasks. The long-term affect of this tool is that children gain confidence in their own abilities, pride in their work, and an associated increase in self-esteem. **Every human being on earth needs to be needed.** The world's greatest joy is *not* being entertained. The greatest joy is to use one's talents to make a difference in the world. I believe we have lost sight of this in our society and it's time to turn the way we deal with children around. Think of how you want your children to evolve. Do you want them to be experienced enough to handle their own lives, or dependent on others to create their experiences for them? A powerful formula for success is: honor the child you **have** and provide him with many opportunities to become more of who he is by using his natural talents.

## DAY FOURTEEN
## Hold the Child's Success in Your Heart

A highly effective way to bring out the best in your child is to **hold her successes in your heart overnight.** You can say:

"I was just thinking about how wonderful you were when we had company yesterday. You said hello to Paul when he arrived at the door and welcomed him in. Did you know that that's one of the best things you can do with other people, show interest in them? It is a powerful skill, and you are learning it. I am so proud of you!"

Saying this **the day after the incident** conveys to the child that her successes are so impressive that you held them in your heart overnight (the way you undoubtedly used to hold infractions in your heart overnight.) Imagine the impact of this delayed response on your child's heart!

Your comments are forging a path in her neural pathways and feeding her self-image positive messages. They also have the effect of giving a huge dose of emotional energy to the behavior you want! This is highly rewarding to the brain, and greatly increases the likelihood that she will repeat the positive behavior.

## My Progress Notes

Obstacles to implementing the ideas in this chapter:

Ways I will overcome the obstacles:

My success story:

## Chapter Three

# Continuing Past the First Two Weeks

### The Point System

Once you feel comfortable with "time in," or immediate positive energy flow for the good behavior; the break, or no energy for negative behavior; and redirection, you may want to institute a point system for rewarding good behavior. (Please note that I regard this as necessary only if you feel the heartfelt appreciation and breaks need supplementing).

Points that can be tracked on a chart add motivation for good behavior for children who are old enough to add and subtract. In a family meeting, you will want to establish **ways to earn points** and **ways to spend them.** Points are granted for all good behaviors, and spent by your child for all privileges. Anything that is not essential for sustaining life is considered a privilege. Food, shelter, clothing (non-designer, unless it's the parents' preference) and education are essentials. Once a point is earned, it is the child's to spend.

**Points are never taken away** for negative behaviors. Remember to avoid responses that would be construed as punishments, as retaliation in some form is a sure result. Discuss the details of timing before you create the points chart. If a trip to the mall or movie is convenient time-wise, the points can be spent on these. If not, you will let the child know when the timing works for you.

Your children will be in charge of their points. Simply tape the point chart on the refrigerator at kid level and tape a pencil attached to a string next to the chart. Whenever your child earns points, she records them herself. When she wants a privilege, your only response is, "Do you have enough points for that? Check your chart!"

# Sophie's Credit Chart: Earning Points

| I earn points by: | points | Monday | Tuesday | Wednesday | Thursday | Friday | Saturday | Sunday |
|---|---|---|---|---|---|---|---|---|
| Cleaning the kitchen | 20 | | | | | | | |
| Taking care of the cat | 10 | | | | | | | |
| Taking out the garbage | 10 | | | | | | | |
| Vacuuming the living room | 20 | | | | | | | |
| Sharing my things with Sis | 30 | | | | | | | |
| Being polite to company | 20 | | | | | | | |
| Not talking back for a day | 20 | | | | | | | |
| Getting ready for school | 20 | | | | | | | |
| Total: | | | | | | | | |

# Sophie's Credit Chart: Spending Points

| I spend points on: | points | Monday | Tuesday | Wednesday | Thursday | Friday | Saturday | Sunday |
|---|---|---|---|---|---|---|---|---|
| Riding my bike—half hour | 10 | | | | | | | |
| Baking cookies | 30 | | | | | | | |
| Time with friends at home | 40 | | | | | | | |
| Time at a friend's house | 40 | | | | | | | |
| PlayStation—half hour | 30 | | | | | | | |
| Tv—half hour | 30 | | | | | | | |
| Trip to an amusement park | 400 | | | | | | | |
| Movie with friends | 100 | | | | | | | |
| Weekly allowance | 30 | | | | | | | |
| Total: | | | | | | | | |

# An Example of a Family's "Earning and Spending" List

## Ways to Earn Points in the Goodman Household

One day of following rules . . . . . . . . . .50 Points
Take out garbage without being asked . . . . . 10
Clear plates without being asked . . . . . . 10
Pick up clothes without being asked . . . . . 10
Pick up living room without being asked . . . . 10
Finish homework without being asked . . . . . 10
Go to bed on time without being asked . . . . 20

## Ways to Spend Points

Extra story . . . . . . . . . . . . . . . . . 10
Video game rental . . . . . . . . . . . . . . 300
Candy . . . . . . . . . . . . . . . . . . . . 25
Baking . . . . . . . . . . . . . . . . . . . . 50
Movie . . . . . . . . . . . . . . . . . . . . 100
Have a friend in . . . . . . . . . . . . . . . 50

## Some other ideas for ways to earn points are:

No arguing or talking back for a morning, an afternoon, or an
    evening (all day is too long for many children)
Telling the truth
Being kind to siblings
Taking care of the pets
Sharing your things without complaining
Cooperating right away when it's time to go somewhere
Good report from school
Brushing teeth, bathing, combing hair without being asked
Getting school things ready the night before
Obeying the babysitter/childcare provider
No whining for a morning, an afternoon, or an evening
Playing well with friends

Speaking nicely when visitors come
Not interrupting parents on the phone
Not interrupting others in conversation
Avoiding dangerous behavior or situations
Allowing others their space
Doing your chores on the weekend
Answering right away when mom or dad calls you
Contributing to the family meeting

## Further ways to spend points are:

(Remember: point spending is subject to parents' schedule and input)

Thirty minutes of TV or video time
Dinner out alone with mom or dad
Shopping trip
Amusement park trip
Special toy or clothing purchase
Money
Trip to the park
Swimming or snow activity, depending on the season
Riding bike in the neighborhood
Sleep-over at home or at friend's house.
Sleep on sibling's bottom bunk
Housekeeping service from mom or dad
Take a friend on a family outing
Cook dinner by yourself, including planning the menu
Overnight trip with family
Day trip with family
Camp out in living room with dad, mom, or both
Electronics (computer, stereo, TV, video games)

These lists are meant to spark your imagination, and are not de-finitive by any means. Your child may have a special interest that would be perfect for the spending list, such as art supplies or go-cart parts. Assign point values according to what works for your family. They will likely need adjusting along the way, as you start to get the "feel" for the way points work for you. Call a family meeting and talk about the adjustments, saying:

"We would like to make the points system work better for our family, so we need your suggestions."

Listen to what the children say, and let their ideas stand whenever possible. If the ideas are not reasonable, stay in the parent place and decide how to allocate points. It's important to keep some "tension" on the points, so that your child does not have so many points stored up that the motivation to earn them is lost.

## Points Earned at School

Intense children often benefit from the consistency of having the same points system at school as at home. Here is a helpful tool for implementing a school/home system of communication about the points.

### Recorded daily by the teacher on this simple chart:

| | Not So Good<br>0 points | Good<br>1 point | Very Good<br>2 points |
|---|---|---|---|
| Teacher Report Form For_____ Date: _____ | | | |
| Keeping hands to self | _____ | _____ | _____ |
| Listening to instructions | _____ | _____ | _____ |
| Playing nicely outside | _____ | _____ | _____ |
| Using indoor voice | _____ | _____ | _____ |
| | | Today's Total: | _____ |

Positive Comments: _____

_____

_____

_____

Your child's teacher can fill out the special school points chart at the end of the day. Parents can facilitate this system by making several weeks' worth of charts for the teacher. Your child can earn ten points at home for each school point. The teacher is asked to provide positive comments to remind him or her that the emphasis is on the good behavior. Be sure that the comments are discussed with the child, and that he receives heartfelt appreciation from you for positive behavior at school. This is a great way for you to affect your child's school day from home!

Note: When asking about your child's school day, be specific. He can't answer, "How was your day?" as the question is just too broad. Instead, ask, "What did you do in math today?" or "Who did you sit with during lunch?" or "What funny thing happened at school today?" These are much more likely to elicit a response, and you just might find your child expanding on the conversation, once it starts!

## Seven Benefits of Present-Moment Parenting

When you have mastered present-moment parenting, you are able to:

1. understand the origin of intensity (the hungry brain)
2. choose to see the positives in the child
3. set firm, welcome boundaries around behavior with a cooperatively designed rule list
4. give heartfelt appreciation for the good behaviors and the lack of breaking rules (time in)
5. give predictable, effective consequences (breaks)
6. teach your values when there is no infraction
7. honor the child you have, and assign grown-up tasks to increase self-esteem
8. deliver heartfelt appreciations after holding successes in your heart, increasing their impact

## Encouragement for You

Give yourself time to integrate all you have read in this guide. Do not feel pressure to have it all down at the end of two weeks, but allow yourself to evolve at your own pace.

And know that **the power of intention** can turn the drama you are experiencing at home into a scene of peace and joy. If you **intend** to be the child's success mentor rather than the behavior police, your effectiveness is assured. Taking that intention to the point of action, you improve the child's behavior, his sense of self, and your relationship. For more on this topic, read *The Power of Intention* by Wayne Dyer.

The excitement of having an intense child in your life does not have to change, but your emotional reactions will definitely change. You will have the thrill of enjoying a spirited kid who has joy for life and whose body has learned **where the energy matches occur: in desired behaviors.** You will also feel more centered and confident as a parent. You will be able to accept credit from friends and family for the improvements, and will have many more pleasant interpersonal moments with your child. In your mind, picture the child as an adult looking back at his relationship with you. Imagine his words as he describes his growing up times with a friend:

"Yeah, I gave my parents a run for their money, but they were always encouraging me. They let me know when I was out of line, but in a respectful way. And they were sure to communicate what they appreciated, so I could learn to act appropriately, feel valued for who I am, and know I was really contributing. I am so grateful to them."

*You and your child*

*are in a*

*win-win situation!*

## My Progress Notes

Obstacles to implementing the ideas in this chapter:

Ways I will overcome the obstacles:

My success story:

## Chapter Four

# Troubleshooting Real Life Challenges

In this chapter, you will read direct responses to specific parents' needs, as they learn to apply present-moment parenting. Enjoy!

### Dealing with Resistance: What If My Child Balks at My Positive Comments?

Many children have trouble receiving a positive comment because they are just not used to heartfelt appreciation coming their way. Most of the feedback they have received from adults has been corrective:

> "Stop that right now."
> "Go to your room (or quiet place at school)."
> "I can't take your attitude one more minute."
> "Can you just do one thing without arguing?"
> "I am busy right now. Don't interrupt me."
> "I never said you could do that."
> "Not again!"
> "NO! I said no, and I meant no."
> "If you do that one more time, I am going to have to
>       ground you."
> "I have to tell you everything a thousand times!"

These comments can download as failures into the child's heart. They all communicate that the child cannot do the right thing. If this sounds like the language your child has been hearing, it is important to note how familiar it must be to his ears and heart. If you suddenly change to saying, "Max, I just love the way you said thank you to Julia's mom so politely today!" you will notice that the child picks up on the difference right away.

It is not necessarily always pleasant for your child to hear positive responses, as they are so different from much of the language to which he is accustomed. But it is very important to continue past this phase by expressing your appreciation of the child's actions. This is necessary to be successful in downloading successes into his heart. Just say,

> "I know this is different from what you are used to hearing, but it's our new way of talking now, and I know you will get used to it."

Communicate that "wild horses couldn't stop you" from pointing out the good things. Children eventually come to accept that this is how the new "family culture" works.

## What If She Refuses to Take a Break?

An intense child frequently refuses to take her breaks. Be ready for this by deciding ahead of time that she will take her break. The clearer you are about the consequence actually occurring, the more secure the child feels. And deciding that you will definitely stop the flow of energy after an infraction will strengthen your efforts significantly. Remember to avoid warnings, reiterations of the rule, and negotiations. These all give energy to behavior you don't want. Use an unemotional, "Broke a Rule. Take a Break." Remind the child that the break doesn't start until she is quiet in the break spot, and that it therefore can't end. She is in charge of the beginning and end of the breaks. Have break spots in every room, and be sure break takes place in your presence. The break is not banishment to another room (a gesture of rejection that downloads as a failure) nor is it punishment. It is simply a deprivation of energy. Turn on the energy as soon as the break has been served well. Say:

"You did a great job of being in break. I am proud of how you handled that!"

If you are consistent in the break expectation, the child will adjust to the new routine. Give it some time. Expect that there may be a window of time between when you have said "Take a break," and the time the child actually takes it. Delivering some kind of heartfelt appreciation during the window, e.g., "You controlled your strong feelings well," often goes a long way toward lifting the child up. Communicate that you are not locked in a power struggle; you still see the good in the child and you still expect the break (consequence) to occur. Use predictive language to encourage the behavior you desire. Say, for example:

"As soon as you are done with your break, will you finish helping me with these cookies?"

## What If There Is an All-Out Tantrum Associated with Breaks?

Give the tantrum no energy, verbal or physical. Accompany the child to the break spot, which communicates that you have decided that the break is going to take place. Take the small child's hand gently, and walk him to the break spot. Use a **safe-hold** in an armless chair if he is swinging or kicking and you are in danger of being hit. The safe-hold: cross the child's arms in front of him and grasp each wrist from behind the chair. Crouch behind the chair below head-butting level. Maintain the hold until the storm passes. Give the child none of your energy. If other children are present, create time in for them by saying something like:

"Sara, I love how you and Amy are cooperating with the blocks! You are taking turns so nicely!"

This not to taunt the child who is taking a break, but to remind him of the rewards of being in time in, as opposed to the lack of energy in taking a break.

With older children who are on the point system, points are frozen until the break is served. No privileges such as friend time, TV, phone time, video games, or computer time are allowed until the break is complete.

As the child becomes accustomed to the routine, she will accept her consequences more readily. Many children evolve to the point that they put themselves in break when necessary! Keep the faith, and use the consequences whenever she steps even an inch over the infraction line. Remember that confusion is very hard on an intense child, and that clarity creates security.

## Dealing with Oppositional Behaviors – Avoiding Triggers

### Here are tips for the language to use with children who oppose you at every turn:

1. Realize that your child has triggers that are beyond his power to overcome. Saying "you have to" and even just "you" can serve as the triggers. Avoid the use of "you" whenever possible. Talk about what "needs to happen" instead. For example, say, "That TV needs to be off so we can enjoy our story."

2. Your child is **compelled** to oppose you. He does not know how to individuate (become fully himself) gently. He **must** tell you that you are wrong in order to know himself as separate from you. Your job is to teach him that he is himself, and no one else can ever be him. Appreciate his unique characteristics, and use his talents in daily living. For example, you might say:

   "You are so good at math. Will you help me figure out the restaurant bill?"
   "You are so good at talking to people. Will you be my phone answerer today?"

"I love how you choose colors. Let's plan the bathroom paint job together!"

Keep in mind that every time you speak to your child, his brain is "watching" for something to oppose. Avoid baiting his brain.

4.   Use language that forwards the action beyond the immediate event. Mention a pleasant activity just ahead or give your child a grown-up task. The former keeps the focus on positives, and the latter supports his individuation by demonstrating that you trust his abilities. For example:

"Brush your teeth right now, or there will be no story tonight."

Replace with: "As soon as you brush your teeth, I'll be ready to read your story."

"Get into the car right now, or we won't be renting that video you wanted."

Replace with: "When we get into the car, I'll need your help with directions to that new video store."

5.   Engage your child's problem-solving abilities rather than telling him what to do. Ask a question instead of delivering a command.
"You just took the last dessert. Now you have to put that back."

Replace with: "Please check around and notice who didn't have dessert yet. What needs to happen next?"

"It's not your turn to talk right now."

Replace with: "What's our rule about letting other people finish speaking?"

This encourages your child to use his own reasoning, which leads him to be less dependent on you and trust more in his own abilities.

6.  Avoid using the child's name at the beginning of a request: Saying "Sam, you need to get your pajamas on right now!" immediately sets his brain up for opposition. His name is a trigger that you want to avoid. Instead, say, "It's 8:00. What do you think happens now?"

    If he plays a "word game" with you, go ahead and entertain him with it for awhile if he is the type of child who can be "jollied" into cooperation. It's fine to use humor with your child, even when it's important that he go to bed. Levity helps people cooperate. But arbitrary treatment causes them to rebel. If he is not the type who can maintain control when you ask him, "What do you think happens now?" just say:

    "Time for bed, everyone! Who gets to turn the TV off tonight? Whose turn is it to turn off the lights? Who's on dog duty this week?"

    This forwards the action and allows the child to cooperate without the challenge of a command.

7.  Pat yourself on the back when you are successful in following the steps above. Give yourself small healthy rewards as you improve, e.g., take a bubble bath; let your schedule include some down time; say "no" to a possible commitment...and feel good about it!

    To keep up your progress with your child, you may want bi-weekly parent coaching appointments to help you keep on track. You'll receive encouragement and credit for the small victories as they emerge. And your coach will help you realize that your home is noticebly more peaceful. Sometimes parent are so wrapped up in problem solving that they forget to notice their own successes!

For me, the best part about being a parent coach is that I get to watch parents take charge of their families, even when it's hard to do. I see them getting the credit from teachers and childcare providers for their children's improved behavior. I see them healing their relationships with their children. And I realize there's no better job in the world!

## Transforming the Difficult Bedtime

Among the parents I coach, one near-universal issue arises at some point: How do we take the pain out of bedtime? Here are some solutions to this often-frustrating everyday issue.

**Set up a family meeting.** Using the same approach that you would with a respected adult, ask your child if she will be available at 7 p.m. on Tuesday to discuss an important issue. She may even want to check to be sure she is available! That's perfectly fine. It's the same process you would go through with a respected colleague. This gives the child a sense of being respected and also infuses a feeling of importance into a troubling issue. I recommend this approach for any topic that needs discussion in your family life.

**Use the meeting to lay out the issue of bedtime squabbles** as objectively as you can. You might say something like, "I have noticed that we are having trouble settling down without an argument at bedtime. I know that when this happens, I get upset, and I imagine that you do, too. I would like to see us have a peaceful bedtime instead, and I am now opening up the discussion to everyone for solutions. What ideas do you have that might help our bedtime go more smoothly?"

**Listen intently to everyone's input,** from the oldest parent to the youngest child. Ask for clarification if something isn't clear. Write suggestions down; this helps everyone feel respected and heard. Remember, caring is defined as giving "close attention." Listening intently is a fabulous way to give everyone close attention. Don't forget to include your own suggestions as you write. Make every effort to incorporate at least one idea from each family member. There may be several good ones, and if you have too many, consider using them on alternate evenings.

**Use present-moment parenting** for bedtime behavior management. Establish the bedtime rules with the child's input. Rules should start with "no": no getting out of bed once the light is out; no asking for more time; no stalling; no negotiating; no whining; no bothering your sister; no crying; no excuses. Children know what the rules are, and the ones they offer will typically be more stringent than yours. Use the child's rules religiously whenever practical, as this creates buy-in, which strengthens the likelihood that the rules will be followed. The clearer the rules, the easier it is for the child to follow them.

**If a bedtime rule is broken, there is an immediate, non-negotiable break.** A gentle, unemotional "Broke a rule. Take a break," is all that is needed. The break should take place in the bed, since that is where the child needs to be, and should last thirty seconds. No energy (no talking, no negotiating, and no engagement of any sort) should be directed to the child during this break. If the child refuses to take a break, take him by the hand and lead him there, with the firm conviction that you have decided that it is bedtime, and there will be no change in your decision. The break begins as soon as the child is calm, and therefore the child can make it end. This system builds a sense of security in the child. It implies that you are in charge, and also that you have complete faith that she can go to sleep on her own.

**Requests for positive behavior should start with, "I need you to"** rather than as questions such as, "Would you please..." or "Would you like to..." which imply the child has a choice. Remember, when you are clear and certain, you are giving your child a huge gift. It may take several nights of this clarity for the child to adjust to the routine, but it will be well worth the effort. Every minute you spend making this work now will pay off significantly in the future. You are teaching your child that she can go to sleep on her own just like a big person. This is very valuable information for her, as it will help her to believe in herself in other areas, too.

**For steps that are completed with cooperation, use heartfelt appreciation** to show that you are noticing and valuing her actions. This creates a powerful time-in which strengthens the desired behavior significantly. You might say, "I see that you have your teeth brushed and are headed for your room. Thank you so much for following our plan, Kristi. Every time you do this, I feel like you are making this house such a wonderful place to live!" Using the formula "When you ___ I feel ___ because ___" for this form of feedback makes remembering how to deliver it much easier.

**Set a definite bedtime.** Younger children should go to bed earlier than the older ones if there is an age difference of two years or more. Usually a half hour is ample time to separate the two bedtimes. If you have three or more children, you may want to make bedtime more uniform so that you assure your adult time at the end of the day. This is very important. Knowing that you, as a single parent or with your spouse or partner, can definitely count on some winding down time helps you to handle the challenges that will come tomorrow. Do not consider this optional. You need your time alone or time together. It is very good modeling for your children, as well. They need to know that time to oneself or as a couple is vital to healthy adult living, and that it also assures that Mom and Dad will be in a good mood tomorrow.

**Include whatever special rituals in the bedtime routine** that the children deem important, and that are acceptable to you. Rituals might be as simple as: wash your face and brush your teeth, take a drink of water, put on pajamas, say goodnight to the fish, read with Mom or Dad, and settle in for sleep. To communicate respect for your child's process, indicate that you value the ritual as much as the child does; be sure to remind her to say goodnight to the fish if she forgets. Rituals are very important for children's transition to the next activity, especially at bedtime. They provide a sense of continuity and comfort, which is vitally important to raising healthy kids. Reading together is my favorite bedtime ritual, as it points out that you value reading and learning, it offers a great opportunity for snuggling, and most important, it truly allows the child to feel your slowed-down, caring energy.

**Requests for extending the reading time will be lovingly denied** when lights-out time has arrived. Make a comment such as, "It makes me so proud to see that you love to read this much, Honey, but tomorrow is another day, and you can read during any free time you have. Now I need to see the light out. Good night. I love you very much."

**Then leave the room and consider the day with children completed** (unless, of course, there is a true illness).

**Note:** Families who are dedicated to more peaceful bedtimes find it fun and very helpful to "rehearse" bedtime. On a Saturday afternoon, you can say, "Let's all go brush our teeth, get into our pajamas, pick out a book to read, and go to bed" and then do it. The kids love it, and it creates maps in their brains that show them exactly what bedtime should look like.

## Present-Moment Parenting with Teens

Chelsea's mom, Nancy, was concerned when she found that her ninth grader had been missing classes at school. She called me for reassurance, fearful that her daughter may be experimenting with drugs. We talked about Eckhardt Tolle's power of now philosophy: "Nothing has ever happened in the past. Nothing will ever happen in the future. Everything happens in the present moment." I encouraged Nancy to keep this present moment in mind. What positives could she see in the girl standing before her right now? When we pay exquisite attention to the present, the future takes care of itself.

After the appointment, I wrote Nancy this follow-up list, reviewing the points we had covered in our conversation:

**Because you are concerned about Chelsea's lying, give heartfelt appreciation** to her every time she tells the truth. Say, "When you fill me in on what's going on, I am so proud of you because it shows me we are building our trust." In fact, use heartfelt appreciation whenever your teenager talks civilly to you! About anything! If you want communication, reward communication.

**Support Chelsea's individuation,** rather than fight it. Use her talents. When writing, say, "Help me with the best way to word this." You can think of many other opportunities to do this.

**Be interested** in her music. Ask her questions about it, and really notice her taste. Listen through her headphones to her favorite song, and comment on the guitar riff that shows particular talent.

**Deep listening** without judgment is the best gift you can give a person, especially a teenager. Just say, "You are feeling really frustrated right now." Don't try to fix the problem. Just listen and reflect the feeling to Chelsea.

**"I trust you"** is music to a teen's ears. Even if you are still in the trust-building stage, use this phrase to plant the idea that establishing trust is possible. It can be about something as small as "I trust you to choose the right words to use with your friend." Or it can be as big as "I trust you to drive the car safely." You will know what to use when.

**Remember that Chelsea is a scientist,** testing to see what stays true over several trials.

**Give her positive feedback** about what a good friend she is, listening and being there when her friend needs her the most.

**Remember that it's a confusing time** when a person has one foot in adulthood and another in childhood. The more supportive you are, the better your relationship will be.

**Have regular family meetings.** Use the first to acknowledge everything good that you notice about each family member. Use subsequent ones to solve problems when necessary.

**Attentive parents are the anti-drug** and the anti-disenfranchisement agent. Even when they can't show it, teens still regard their parents as the biggest influence in their lives. Keep this in mind, and never waver from your role as your child's life guide, even when peers seem to be their only influence.

**Keep the sense of belonging** focused on Chelsea's place in the family, so the need to find it with peers is not as strong.

I have confidence that this will just be a phase. Nancy has done a wonderful job and Chelsea is so fortunate to have her as her mom. She is a parent who really cares, and it shows.

## Preventing Kids from Being Over-Scheduled

Over-scheduling has been a recurrent topic in many parent coaching sessions I've recently had with clients. Here are some of the concerns expressed by parents and hints about ways to prevent getting your child too involved:

**Is it OK to stay home with a twenty-month-old, where he only sees adults and doesn't have playdates?** Before the age of two or three, it's perfectly fine for adults to be the primary contacts with a child. Often very young children need developmental time before they are able to behave appropriately with other children. Although most children are exposed to peers in childcare at a much earlier age, it's perfectly fine to start introducing them to their peers when they are three. One big advantage to keeping your child close to home is may be sick less frequently than he would be if he were exposed to other children!

**Should three-year-olds take music and swimming lessons?** The age and developmental stage of the child should be the first consideration in making these decisions. A three-year-old can readily take swimming lessons, but the expectations of him in the class should be minimal. If he enjoys the water and is learning new skills without anxiety, the lessons can continue. If he's frightened, refusing to participate or do what the instructor says, feel free to wait a year or two before introducing swimming lessons again.

**Is it all right to let your child quit a sport or activity?** I realize that many parents are worried that they may be raising a "quitter" if they allow their children to stop participating in a sport or musical activity. Please keep in mind that childhood is a time for exploring a variety of possibilities. Children need to be free to say yes to something, try it, and decide if they are enjoying themselves. If the activity is stressful for the child, or if she just doesn't enjoy it, it's perfectly fine to stop and look around to see what the other choices might be. The younger the child, the more fluid the decisions can be. As she grows up and commits herself to high school activities, she will likely remain more loyal to them. By then she has a better-defined sense of self, and more decision-making skills. She'll still need your guidance, and be sure to encourage her to listen to what her heart says when she's making a decision. It's more preferable to grow up learning how to honor one's true self than to continue in an activity because of others' expectations and desires.

**How many nights a week should we schedule an activity?** This all depends on the age of the child, her energy level, and her school demands. If a child is very interested in sports, music, or dance, and wants to participate, it's wonderful to offer the opportunity. But be sure you limit the time spent in outside activities, so that her life maintains its balance. Kids need down time in order to develop their imaginations. They need to study the clouds and go looking for interesting rocks. They need to just spend time musing. If your child rarely has quiet alone time, be sure to make an effort to provide it. And this should be time without the computer, TV or video games...just quiet alone time. If your very active child is always on the go, don't be concerned, but do create quiet family time, so that he becomes accustomed to unscheduled periods every week. If you encounter your normally active child spending time "doing nothing," appreciate it. It's a necessary thing, something to be honored and protected.

**At what age can children decide on activities for themselves?** When you decide to offer a new activity to your child, give him time to get used to it, and then listen for signs of satisfaction or disenchantment. Avoid doing too much to influence his decision. Offering small encouragements to stay involved is fine, but pushing is never a good idea. Do not look at your child's sports, music, or dance as your way to gain self-esteem. Such things should always be about the child, as it's his life. If you allow him to decide what he'd like to spend his time doing, he learns a very important skill: listening to his inner voice, and answering his true desires. He'll likely change interests many times throughout childhood, and the freedom to do so is vital to his healthy development. If you have spent money enrolling your child in an activity, let the money go if the child decides not to continue. It's still well spent, as the child has gained good information about himself and the activity. He has also gained decision-making skills while he still has you as a resource.

**What signs of stress tell us that children are over-scheduled?** Children who are tired all the time, are frequently argumentative, and act reluctant to participate in the simplest activities, are often letting their adults know that they are over-scheduled. You might ask the child if life feels like "too much" but don't be surprised to hear her say no. She will feel a pull from peers or from within herself to stay involved with her activities. If you determine that the stress outweighs the benefits, exercise your parental role and make a decision to have her cut back. And think of ways to reduce the overall stress in her life as well. Stress is a significant health concern in children, and they need adults to help them return to balanced lives. Do not fear letting the coach, dance instructor, or band director down. It's your job first and foremost to protect your child from being overstressed. Schoolwork and family time should take priority, and everything else needs to fall into place behind them.

## What Your Child Can't Tell You

You have probably heard the saying, **"All behavior is communication."** The more I think about this, the more I see how relevant it is to raising children. I want everyone to emblazon this where they will see it every day. **Children misbehave because they lack the communication skills and insight to tell us what's really happening.** It's our job to **look beyond the behavior** to the root feelings.

When a child whines, it is not because she likes the sound of whining. It's because she lacks the maturity and experience to say, "Mom, Dad, I am frustrated right now because you are asking me to hurry for school, but I am a kid and I'm just slower." Instead, she'll exhibit all kinds of unwanted behaviors: whining, delaying, arguing, and even getting physically aggressive.

When a grade-schooler refuses to do his homework, it's not likely that he is simply lazy. **His behavior is communicating that he is discouraged in some way.** Our first impulse as parents is to **make him see** that he needs to get the work done so he can be successful. We remind, cajole, threaten, and eventually explode. A much more helpful first impulse is to determine what to do about the discouragement.

When a teenager doesn't listen to our advice, it's not because he is just being a jerk. **His behavior is communicating that he is in a new phase of development.** He needs to make his own decisions, and we are inadvertently calling him incompetent whenever we advise him. He takes it as an insult every time we make a suggestion. He isn't able to say, "Mom, Dad, I appreciate that you care about me, and that you are wiser than I am. But I need to make these decisions myself because I am becoming a young adult, and that's what young adults do. Please bear with me as I struggle and even fail sometimes." Instead, he leaves the house in a huff, giving the door an extra hard slam for emphasis. We would be much better off if our first impulse was to support him in his decision-making, rather than to tell him what to do.

**If you want cooperative behavior from your kids, take a shortcut by training your mind to see what's beneath the behavior.** Practice seeing your child's innocence first, and working to understand what lies beneath the foul language, the time spent with the door locked, and the "interesting" style of dress. You will find a vulnerable, changing child who simply doesn't have insight yet. It's our job as adults to gain this insight and act accordingly.

Rather than exhibit anger over disrespectful behavior, acknowledge there's an emotion that the child cannot express directly lying just under the surface. Kids get hurt a lot easier than most adults realize, so they are compelled to protect their tender hearts by lashing out. If we don't give them cause to protect themselves, by utilizing our clear view of what's really going on, they won't have to be so defensive.

**So the next time you see a child "acting out," ask yourself what's being communicated.** It will be an emotion that the child is too young or too immature to express directly, such as feelings of hurt, frustration, disappointment, hopelessness, or something else you can help to identify. Then address the child in those terms, rather than with your own irritation. Say, "You seem upset. Want to tell me what's up?" or "How about you take some time in your own room until you feel better and we can talk?" or "I remember being your age and feeling that same way. Sit down, and let's try to make this better together." You'll be getting to the root emotion rather than placing judgment on the child's behavior. Congratulations! You are on the shortcut to better communication and better behavior with your child.

## When Your Child Lies

Lying is a topic that really gets to many parents. It's so easy to go to the "fear place" when your four-year-old experiments with telling you something that is obviously not true.

### It's a Normal Phase

First, realize that it's a developmental milestone for kid to lie. Children do it because they figure out that there is such a thing as saying something that isn't true. It's that simple. They are not morally bad when they lie; they are just scientists testing their newfound information. "I am six years old," coming from a three-year-old is simply an experiment with saying "I am six years old." It comes from a new realization that everything one says may not really be so. When kids make a new discovery, they try it out. Lying is no different.

### No Energy

Your best response to your child's lie is to either joke with the child and say, "Six? I thought you were twelve!" or simply state, "You're three, remember?" The other alternative is to just smile and let it go. This is not deceitful lying. The thing you don't want to do is give your emotional energy to the lies, which would assure you that the lying continues.

When children get older, you can tell when the intent is to truly deceive in order to avoid responsibility. All children do it, so please don't think your child is unique. Again, your best response is to not over-react. Keep the experimenting scientist in mind, and simply say, "We know you didn't brush your teeth. I'll meet you in the bedroom for a story as soon as you have them all shiny." This last part is called "forwarding the action." It helps kids realize you are not buying their story, and that you are not giving the lie any energy by staying stuck on it. You are moving on to the next thought, and the next activity, and you expect they will follow.

### Social Lying

As they move into the middle-school years, you might find your child in a dilemma about when to tell a small white lie in order to avoid hurting a friend's feelings. She will get invited to her best friend's house immediately after accepting an invitation to the home of a lesser-known peer. Let her struggle with this one; don't jump in to resolve it right away. And don't think there is only one right answer. The desire to be with her best buddy overrides everything else at this age, so she'll likely choose her best friend. You might see it go either way, but again, try not to get too involved in the outcome. Natural consequences are great teachers in these situations, and kids' relationships are quite fluid.

Your child may snub another child, but three weeks later be her close friend. Allowing them to work it out while you are there to listen and offer support is really the best strategy. Give your child heartfelt appreciation whenever she makes a good decision, and let it go if you think it's questionable. It's all part of the growing-up process. You might want to talk about empathy, but do it at another time. When the situation is ripe, the emotions are usually too high to make a point about social graces.

### Tap Your Child's Experience

Ask your child what he learned about his last experience with lying. Maybe someone else lied to him, and he wants to say how that felt. This is perfect soil for planting empathy. And don't expect him to be perfect with it right away. Learning empathy is a process, not a one-time lesson.

### Grow Truth-Telling

Be sure to give your heartfelt appreciation every time your child tells the truth! For example, say, "When you tell me the truth about throwing rocks outside, I really appreciate it, because it shows me how honest you are! Now take your break, and then we'll go put those rocks back where they belong."

### Be the Young Scientist's Laboratory Findings

As a rule of thumb, under-reacting to lying while stating what you know is true (or is likely true) will be your approach to lying. Just keep the scientists in mind, and give them the findings you want them to discover. Your response to lying should be an unemotional correction with no energy. And keep in mind that kids are learning everything from you, so if you want them to learn honesty, exhibit honesty!

## Look for Sensory Integration Issues

Parents frequently feel mystified by their children's extreme behavior, not realizing that sensory issues are at play. These hidden factors are very often the reason for tantrums, attempts to control others, the use of harsh language, and melt-downs. Kids with sensory integration disorder have difficulty integrating what their senses tell them, so they can't move on to the next activity. A child with auditory sensory issues, for example, is unable to readily integrate sounds, which makes even ordinary sounds upsetting to her. This can cause her to be highly distracted in a classroom setting, but better at home, where the noise level is lower. Such a child might get off the bus and collapse into tears of pain and frustration, leaving her parents confused and frustrated. The noise on the bus has overwhelmed her so she becomes totally out of control by the time she arrives home.

Children who cover their ears when a train goes by or in response to other loud noises, and who then exhibit anger, rage, and disrespectful behavior, may be suffering from auditory sensory disorder. They hear the sounds of everyday life much more acutely than does the average person, and they are essentially tortured by those sounds. "Normal" sounds can be equivalent to the booming of bombs going off all around them. No wonder they melt down.

Some children have visual sensory integration disorder. They are extremely sensitive to light, and often come totally unglued in a room with fluorescent lighting. These children can see the lights vibrating at a speed that is undetectable to most people. This results in utterly understandable misbehavior in the classroom.

Other children have tactile sensitivity. They insist on soft fabrics, and can't stand the tags in their clothes or the seams in their socks. They are often extremely picky about the length of their pants or sleeves. If the tactile sensitivity affects the mouth, the children can't stand the texture of certain foods. They will be very picky eaters, again often mystifying their parents.

It's never a good idea to try to talk your child out of being particular about sensory sensitivity, or to punish him for tantrums related to sensory input. Occupational therapists in private practice can help your child with sensory issues, teaching his body to more readily integrate what his senses tell him. Ask your family doctor or pediatrician for an OT recommendation. And try to accommodate your child's needs as they arise. He truly can't make himself accept loud noises, tags in clothes, highly textured foods, or fluorescent lights by force of will. He needs professional intervention to overcome these obstacles to living a happy life, and just as important, he needs your understanding. You won't be spoiling your child by buying soft clothes, helping him protect his ears, or letting the broccoli go. In these cases, accommodations are simply compassionate.

## A Loving Mom's Victory

Belinda is the devoted mother of a home-schooled, brilliant seven-year-old. Her son, Andrew, is inquisitive, determined, and always ahead of the game. In fact, Andrew is a very powerful child who has so many leadership qualities that he struggles to understand why he is not in charge of both his family's life and all his interactions with his peers. When, for example, he's disagreed with his mom's restaurant choice, this little boy, one who is quite sensitive to ambient noise, has said, "How would you like me to go where you want to go, and hurt my ears?" (because the place will be too noisy). On other occasions, he's said, "If we go with Grandma and Grandpa, there will be four happy people and one unhappy person."

Andrew's impulsive behavior and attempts at controlling his environment, like making his parents and grandparents cave in to his desires, has often proved overwhelming for everyone; Belinda has found herself in an increasingly exhausting battle to respond to him. When things haven't gone well, Belinda has employed her default nagging, yelling, pleading, explaining, and punishing techniques, all to little avail. Belinda recognized that she needed help dealing with her challenging child.

After two coaching sessions, Belinda began to see that *it's much better for Andrew if she holds the line on her decisions.* Instead of pleading, explaining, and teaching, she's learned to remain very calm and to give him a choice, such as: "You can go with us and act politely, or you can eat dinner here alone in your room." On one particular occasion, Andrew quickly chose the restaurant option. As it turned out, they were seated in the noisiest spot of the dining room, and Andrew never complained a bit. In fact, Belinda realized by reading his body language that Andrew was relieved when she didn't allow him to take the reins regarding the restaurant decision. This is a perfect example of how "staying in the parent place" results in better behavior and smoother interactions. Powerful kids **are** relieved when their parents don't give in. Deep inside, they know their parents need to make decisions, and when that happens smoothly and without struggle, they feel secure and can let go of trying to control the situation. Belinda's sticking with her plan and offering Andrew a choice opened the door for Andrew's cooperation.

In another incident, Belinda took Andrew shopping for a birthday present for his twin friends who were turning nine. When Andrew was confronted with the fact that the shopping trip was not going to involve buying anything for him, he melted down. "You don't care about me! Why should we pay attention to just them?" he shouted. Belinda was able to realize that giving energy to Andrew's nonsense was not going to get better behavior from him, so she got creative. As Andrew was having his tantrum in the very crowded checkout line, Belinda excused herself from the line for a minute, reminding Andrew to take a take a break while simultaneously holding their place. Staying close enough to assure Andrew's safety, Belinda wisely removed herself from the fray, even as she gave Andrew the "grown-up task" of holding their place in line.

When they got to the car, Andrew launched a similar tantrum. Belinda calmly explained that he could go to the birthday party if he was willing to take his good attitude with him, or he could miss the party and go home. She didn't argue, nag, or ask him why he couldn't improve his attitude; she just offered him a straightforward choice. Good attitude = go to the party. Not-so-good attitude = go home. Belinda was prepared to take Andrew home, being wise enough to only offer choices she was willing to carry out.

Andrew opted to take his good attitude to the party. And when he got there, he held himself together in a way that caused Belinda to stare in amazement. As the children were gathered in a raucous group, she stood ten feet away and watched in awe as Andrew stood up in the crowd, opened his mouth to say something he shouldn't, thought a minute, closed his mouth, and sat down.

A few moments later, a high-energy girl with whom Andrew was very familiar approached him, announcing, "Your present stinks!" Andrew refused the bait, further amazing his mom.

When reflecting on Belinda and Andrew's story, it's just as important to examine what caused Andrew's good behavior as it is to look at what causes his negative behavior.

Here are some things to think about:

**With Belinda's new parenting, Andrew's body reacts in a new, healthier way.**

As Belinda remembers to avoid matching negative energy by nagging Andrew, she opens the door to Andrew's relaxation around conflict. She simply offers him a choice, or says, "Broke a Rule. Take a break." For Andrew, there's no more of the adrenaline rush that formerly fueled arguments. Andrew's neurological system, once used to the physiological response that resulted from confrontation, now enjoys peace. His ability to comply with Belinda's requests is greatly enhanced when the extreme peaks of tantrum-inducing emotion are not part of his everyday routine. Further, he feels more secure because of the predictability of his mom's calm response and his planned-ahead break. In fact, his new physiological response is directly related to the break-taking behavior that they have rehearsed in advance. The rules and "break spots" were established during a family meeting, so there is no surprise in the interaction. Instead of experiencing an adrenaline rush, Andrew's body knows to respond calmly when his mother remains calm and reminds him of their break plan. He is even showing signs of reminding himself, as evidenced by his extreme self-control at the birthday party!

### Belinda has gained confidence.

The more Belinda witnesses Andrew's successes, the more deeply entrenched her new responses become. She sees Andrew's ability to control his strong urges rising from the ashes of their formerly tempestuous relationship, and she knows that *she causes the improvements.*

For example, Belinda realized that Andrew was greatly relieved when she took the reins during the restaurant decision. She knew she was helping to create this very positive emotional response in her child, which helped her remember to repeat that "rein-taking" behavior. Belinda's rein-taking was directly linked to Andrew's increasingly positive behavior. When he realized that his mother was holding the reins, he was freed up to exert his own self-control. He even built on his sense of self-control when standing to speak at the party and thinking better of it, and by refusing to get involved when a child confronted him with a direct insult about his gift. Andrew's response amazed Belinda and instilled a degree of pride she hadn't felt for a long time.

Belinda's trusting Andrew to take his break in line at the store while serving a grown-up purpose (holding their place in the line) enhanced his sense of his own usefulness. Note that he went from being furious about not getting a present to being helpful in a new way, all in a span of a few moments. Experiencing appropriate power is vital for intelligent children. Giving Andrew a grown-up task was the best thing Belinda could have done to lift him to a higher level of confidence in his own abilities. Further, Belinda's trust in Andrew enhanced her own confidence in her parenting skills. She walked away feeling victorious.

Please note the phrases used in the discussion of Belinda's experience:

"She knows that she causes the improvements."

"She knew she was helping to create this very positive emotional response in her child..."

"Andrew's response amazed Belinda and instilled a degree of pride she hadn't felt for a long time."

"Belinda's trust in Andrew enhanced her own confidence in her parenting skills."

If you are the parent of a bright, intense child, you know how hard it is to stay ahead of him or her. Hopefully, Belinda's story has inspired you, and has given you the knowledge that you don't need to be stuck in a power struggle with your child, alternately playing the heavy and giving in. You deserve to have control of your family life ... and you can have it! With the approach that Belinda has learned, you'll be well on your way to success, relief, and confidence.

## My Progress Notes

Obstacles to implementing the ideas in this chapter:

Ways I will overcome the obstacles:

My success story:

## Chapter Five

# Using Restorative Justice with Present-Moment Parenting

When the 30-second break doesn't seem like "enough of a consequence" for the more serious infraction, you can teach your children restorative justice, which puts the emphasis on repairing the harm caused by the offender. Restorative justice includes all those involved in the incident, which is healing for the offender and the victim. The offender doesn't have to live with the mark of the offense in his or her heart. The victim has her sense of fairness restored when the offender takes steps to make amends.

These techniques can be used to resolve issues between siblings, peers, and children and adults. As parents, you'll "work yourselves out of a job" by teaching children to resolve conflict on their own. No more spending your time refereeing squabbles and trying to reason with upset kids. The offender will take a break immediately after the infraction, and when the feelings have settled down a bit, you'll use the present moment to employ restorative justice. And just as with taking a break in the face of an infraction, you will set the example by using restorative justice yourself.

First, use a family meeting to discuss restorative justice, teach it to the children, and rehearse it. Only employ this technique after teaching it directly:

1. The offender and the offended sit face to face. The offender tells what it felt like to offend. ("I was really mad and it

felt good to hit you because you took my stuff and wouldn't give it back.")

2. The offended tells what it felt like to be hurt. ("It really, really hurt when you hit me. My arm is still sore and swollen. My feelings are hurt, too, because you shouldn't do that!")

3. Together they decide how to make up for the offense. The conversation might go like this:

"I think you should do my after-dinner chores for a week."

"A week? That's too long for a little hit on the arm. How about four days?"

"How about five? And I'll help on a little on the fifth day."

"OK."

With this exercise, you have taught the children that:

· they, and not you, are in charge of resolving their conflicts. You will give no emotional energy for negativity.

· justice can be restored, and the infraction doesn't have to stay with either of them.

· they have a known, predictable method for resolving issues and are expected to use it.

Just as with taking breaks, no privileges will be allowed until the mutually agreed-upon solution has been decided.

In the case of stealing from a store or damaging someone's property, the same procedure applies. The child sits with the adult owner, says what it felt like to offend, and listens as the owner expresses his feelings on the incident. Together they decide what will occur to make amends. The child may have a hard time accepting the agreement. If it's reasonable, support him or her in accepting it.

With rehearsal in advance, you have greatly increased the chance of compliance. By employing restorative justice in the face of significant conflict yourself, you will also support your children in their success. You now have an established system for dealing with conflict in your family. It's up to you to enforce restorative justice whenever a disagreement results in severe emotional or physical injury. With the use of this calm, low-energy approach, you'll have yet another great reason to feel proud of your family as they resolve issues by coming together as skilled problem solvers!

## My Progress Notes

Obstacles to implementing the ideas in this chapter:




Ways I will overcome the obstacles:




My success story:

# Resources for Parents

Clarke, Jean Illsley, Connie Dawson, and David J. Bredehoft. *How Much Is Enough?: Everything You Need to Know to Steer Clear of Overindulgence and Raise Likeable, Responsible, and Respectful Children.* New York: Marlowe & Company, 2003. Visit www.overindulgence.info for more information.

Dyer, Wayne. *The Secrets of the Power of Intention: Learning to Co-Create Your World Your Way.* Carlsbad, CA: Hay House, 2004. Visit www.hayhouse.com for more information.

Glasser, Howard and Jennifer Easley. *Transforming the Difficult Child: The Nurtured Heart Approach.* Tucson, AZ: Nurtured Heart Publications, 1999.
Visit www.difficultchild.com for more information.

Levine, Mel, M.D. *The Myth of Laziness.* New York: Simon and Schuster, 2003.
Visit www.allkindsofminds.org for more information.

Tolle, Eckhardt. *The Power of Now.* Novato, CA: New World Library, 1999.
Visit www.eckharttolle.com for more information.
Visit www.nurturedheart.com to order the audio CD of Tina coaching a mother of three: *"60 Minutes with Parent Coach Tina Feigal."*

Also downloadable at www.nurturedheart.com are guides for teachers that correlate wth this book: *The Pocket Teacher Coach: Early Childhood* and *The Pocket Teacher Coach: Grades 1-6.*

The Institute of Heartmath.
Visit www.heartmath.com for more information.

# Personal Parent Coaching
## for Your Use

### Downloading Powerful Successes by Including Feeling Language

| When you___<br>because___ | I feel___ |
|---|---|
| clean up<br>it helps mom's day go better. | rested |
| tell me about your social events<br>you're sharing your life with me. | close to you |
| say "OK" when I ask you something<br>there's no screaming. | relieved |
| go to bed when asked<br>I don't have to ask more than once. | listened to |
| control your strong feelings<br>you worked hard to help us get along. | my heart gets so big |
| put your hat and coat on<br>we get Sister to school on time. | so excited |
| surprised me by doing your chores<br>I know you are trying to please me. | important and loved |
| help your brother with a game<br>you are listening to my request. | respected |
| hang up your jacket<br>we don't have to pick up after you. | appreciative |
| share your toys<br>I see the generous person you are. | proud |
| start homework without being told<br>we'll get to do other things together. | excited |

## Sophie's Credit Chart

| I earn points by: | Points | Monday | Tuesday | Wednesday | Thursday | Friday | Saturday |
|---|---|---|---|---|---|---|---|
| Cleaning the kitchen | 20 | | | | | | |
| Taking care of the cat | 10 | | | | | | |
| Taking out the garbage | 10 | | | | | | |
| Vacuuming the living room | 20 | | | | | | |
| Sharing my things with Sis | 30 | | | | | | |
| Being polite to company | 20 | | | | | | |
| Not talking back for a day | 20 | | | | | | |
| Getting ready for school | 20 | | | | | | |
| **TOTAL:** | | | | | | | |

88

## Sophie's Credit Chart

| I spend points on: | Points | Monday | Tuesday | Wednesday | Thursday | Friday | Saturday |
|---|---|---|---|---|---|---|---|
| Riding my bike—half hour | 10 | | | | | | |
| Baking cookies | 30 | | | | | | |
| Time with friends at home | 40 | | | | | | |
| Time at a friend's house | 40 | | | | | | |
| PlayStation—half hour | 30 | | | | | | |
| TV—half hour | 30 | | | | | | |
| Trip to amusement park | 400 | | | | | | |
| Movie with friends | 100 | | | | | | |
| Weekly allowance | 30 | | | | | | |
| TOTAL: | | | | | | | |

## Additional Exercises for Communicating Values

• The value:_____

How I communicated it:_____

_____

When I communicated:    _____After the infraction
                        _____When things were calm

• The value:_____

_____

How I communicated it:_____

_____

When I communicated:    _____After the infraction
                        _____When things were calm

• The value:_____

How I communicated it:_____

_____

When I communicated:    _____After the infraction
                        _____When things were calm

• The value:_____

_____

How I communicated it:_____

_____

When I communicated:    _____After the infraction
                        _____When things were calm

Describe an incident where you let your values go:

_____

_____

_____

_____

_____

_____

_____

_____

_____

How would you change it? _____

_____

_____

_____

_____

_____

_____

_____

_____

_____

_____

_____

_____

Describe an incident where you let your values go:

_____

_____

_____

_____

_____

_____

_____

_____


How would you change it? _____

_____

_____

_____

_____

_____

_____

_____

_____

_____

_____

_____

Describe an incident where you let your values go:

_____

_____

_____

_____

_____

_____

_____

_____

How would you change it? _____

_____

_____

_____

_____

_____

_____

_____

_____

_____

_____

## Making Heartfelt Appreciation Effective

| When you... | I feel... | because... |
|---|---|---|
|  |  |  |
|  |  |  |
|  |  |  |
|  |  |  |
|  |  |  |
|  |  |  |

## Making Heartfelt Appreciation Effective

| When you... | I feel... | because... |
|---|---|---|
|  |  |  |
|  |  |  |
|  |  |  |
|  |  |  |
|  |  |  |
|  |  |  |

# Credit Chart for _____

# Earning Points

| I earn points by: | points | Monday | Tuesday | Wednesday | Thursday | Friday | Saturday | Sunday |
|---|---|---|---|---|---|---|---|---|
| Cleaning the kitchen | 20 | | | | | | | |
| Taking care of the cat | 10 | | | | | | | |
| Taking out the garbage | 10 | | | | | | | |
| Vacuuming the living room | 20 | | | | | | | |
| Sharing my things with Sis | 30 | | | | | | | |
| Being polite to company | 20 | | | | | | | |
| Not talking back for a day | 20 | | | | | | | |
| Getting ready for school | 20 | | | | | | | |
| Total: | | | | | | | | |

# Credit Chart for _____    Spending Points

| I spend points on: | points | Monday | Tuesday | Wednesday | Thursday | Friday | Saturday | Sunday |
|---|---|---|---|---|---|---|---|---|
| Riding my bike—half hour | 10 | | | | | | | |
| Baking cookies | 30 | | | | | | | |
| Time with friends at home | 40 | | | | | | | |
| Time at a friend's house | 40 | | | | | | | |
| PlayStation—half hour | 30 | | | | | | | |
| Tv—half hour | 30 | | | | | | | |
| Trip to an amusement park | 400 | | | | | | | |
| Movie with friends | 100 | | | | | | | |
| Weekly allowance | 30 | | | | | | | |
| Total: | | | | | | | | |

# Daily Reminder Slips

The positives are where my true power lies. I download a positive into my child's heart at every opportunity. I use "When you__I feel__because__" to add intensity.

The positives are where my true power lies. I download a positive into my child's heart at every opportunity. I use "When you__I feel__because__" to add intensity.

The positives are where my true power lies. I download a positive into my child's heart at every opportunity. I use "When you__I feel__because__" to add intensity.

The positives are where my true power lies. I download a positive into my child's heart at every opportunity. I use "When you__I feel__because__" to add intensity.

The positives are where my true power lies. I download a positive into my child's heart at every opportunity. I use "When you__I feel__because__" to add intensity.

The positives are where my true power lies. I download a positive into my child's heart at every opportunity. I use "When you__I feel__because__" to add intensity.

# Daily Reminder Slips

The positives are where my true power lies. I download a positive into my child's heart at every opportunity. I use "When you___I feel___because___" to add intensity.

The positives are where my true power lies. I download a positive into my child's heart at every opportunity. I use "When you___I feel___because___" to add intensity.

The positives are where my true power lies. I download a positive into my child's heart at every opportunity. I use "When you___I feel___because___" to add intensity.

The positives are where my true power lies. I download a positive into my child's heart at every opportunity. I use "When you___I feel___because___" to add intensity.

The positives are where my true power lies. I download a positive into my child's heart at every opportunity. I use "When you___I feel___because___" to add intensity.

The positives are where my true power lies. I download a positive into my child's heart at every opportunity. I use "When you___I feel___because___" to add intensity.

# Daily Reminder Slips

The positives are where my true power lies. I download a positive into my child's heart at every opportunity. I use "When you__I feel__because__" to add intensity.

The positives are where my true power lies. I download a positive into my child's heart at every opportunity. I use "When you__I feel__because__" to add intensity.

The positives are where my true power lies. I download a positive into my child's heart at every opportunity. I use "When you__I feel__because__" to add intensity.

The positives are where my true power lies. I download a positive into my child's heart at every opportunity. I use "When you__I feel__because__" to add intensity.

The positives are where my true power lies. I download a positive into my child's heart at every opportunity. I use "When you__I feel__because__" to add intensity.

The positives are where my true power lies. I download a positive into my child's heart at every opportunity. I use "When you__I feel__because__" to add intensity.

# Broke a Rule Notes

BROKE A RULE.

TAKE A BREAK.

BROKE A RULE.

TAKE A BREAK.

BROKE A RULE.

TAKE A BREAK.

BROKE A RULE.

TAKE A BREAK.

BROKE A RULE.

TAKE A BREAK.

BROKE A RULE.

TAKE A BREAK.

BROKE A RULE.

TAKE A BREAK.

BROKE A RULE.

TAKE A BREAK.

# Broke a Rule Notes

BROKE A RULE.

TAKE A BREAK.

BROKE A RULE.

TAKE A BREAK.

BROKE A RULE.

TAKE A BREAK.

BROKE A RULE.

TAKE A BREAK.

BROKE A RULE.

TAKE A BREAK.

BROKE A RULE.

TAKE A BREAK.

BROKE A RULE.

TAKE A BREAK.

BROKE A RULE.

TAKE A BREAK.

**Broke a Rule Notes**

BROKE A RULE.

TAKE A BREAK.

BROKE A RULE.

TAKE A BREAK.

BROKE A RULE.

TAKE A BREAK.

BROKE A RULE.

TAKE A BREAK.

BROKE A RULE.

TAKE A BREAK.

BROKE A RULE.

TAKE A BREAK.

BROKE A RULE.

TAKE A BREAK.

BROKE A RULE.

TAKE A BREAK.

# About the Author

Tina Feigal, M.S., Ed. is a passionate parent coach, trainer for professionals, and founder of the Center for the Challenging Child, LLC. Since 2000, she has developed her coaching and training business, working with people from all over the English-speaking world. Tina credits her three sons, Ben, Jordan, and Jacob, for being her main teachers and for inspiring her to help parents and their kids grow the best possible relationships. In fact, before she earned her master's degree in education, Tina received her Ph.D. in "Challenging Child Studies and Management" from Jordan, and for this she is ever grateful. (Jordan's now a child therapist!)

Tina is the parenting coach for Minneapolis-St. Paul's NBC affiliate, KARE 11 TV, offering on-screen parenting tips. She also hosts a parenting web forum at www.kare11.com. Tina offers a monthly e-newsletter, Nurturing News, to thousands of parents nationwide through her web site, www.nurturedheart.com. In addition, she speaks at conferences all over the U.S. to a mix of audiences, addressing parents, teachers, social workers, clergy, foster and adoptive parents, childcare providers, and members of associations who work for children's causes.

Tina believes that putting healing in the hands of adults who love and teach intense and challenging children is the best possible "model" for making life easier with and for these children. Who better to cause the improvements than the very parents and teachers who raise and teach such children? She dedicates her life to seeing parents and teachers become empowered by employing positive techniques that really work!